Brian's
Last Ride

MARIANNE CURTIS

Published by Emerald Publications

ISBN: 1481818546
ISBN-13: 978-1481818544

DEDICATION

In memory of Brian

This story is based on actual events.
With the exception of the victim's name, all other names have been
changed to protect the identity of those involved.

INTRODUCTION

Winnipeg Free Press, Monday, September 24, 1984, Page 4

24 September 1984 – *A collision between two dirt bikes Friday night has resulted in the death of a 14year old youth from Landmark. RCMP said Brian Mark Kauenhofen was killed when he rear-ended a second dirt bike driven by another youth and a female passenger. The other two riders escaped with minor injuries.*

I closed my eyes. I could feel the color seep from my face. My guts churned and I fought the urge to vomit. This was the first time I lay eyes on a news article about this particular accident; yet here I was staring at it, mesmerized by the straightforward news brief.

I am not sure what compelled me to Google this incident – twenty-eight years after the fact. As a matter of fact, when I typed Brian's name into the search engine I was confident (but hopeful) that my search would come up empty. But it didn't. Details were scarce but there it was in black and white - a brief description from one of the worst nights of my young life.

The words were unpretentious, obviously from a Royal Canadian Mounted Police (RCMP) press release. There were three of us present that night but only one of our names appeared in the article. This came as no surprise - we were all under age and protected by law. The only reason Brian's name was made public was because the tragedy cost his life.

At the time and still, nearly thirty years later, not many knew of my involvement in the incident. To the public (and the tiny community where it happened) I was just a "female passenger"; faceless and nameless. Unfortunately, I knew the truth and along with it, I carried a lot of shame. I was there and I still believe I was responsible. I still have the memories; they've faded a little, but the cause-and-effect of the night remains active in my life today. I am frightened to take chances, I am afraid to meet new people, and sometimes, I genuinely believe that I am bad luck, especially if something horrible happens to someone in my life. This has made me shut down and avoid even fun, harmless situations out of fear because I learned the hard way that having fun could be costly.

Over the course of three decades I have learned that all three of us were innocent victims. My guilt and shame was misguided. The collision was completely preventable, but it was still an accident. Guilt is a heavy burden to carry an entire lifetime so this realization brings me great relief.

I got something else out of the article, something unexpected. I finally had a date – September 21, 1984. In the heat of the crisis and the subsequent handling of the incident, I failed to remember the specific date that all our lives changed. I remember details from that night like it was yesterday but the actual date it happened, I couldn't have told you – until now.

I may have forgotten the exact date of the incident but I have never forgotten the details surrounding the night that Brian took his last ride.

SEPTEMBER 21, 1984

The night Brian died still haunts me. Due to the ill-fated events from that fall night in 1984, I will forever believe fourteen-years-old is too young for someone to take their last breathe. Just like sixteen-years-old is too young to emotionally deal with the ramifications of such an incident; especially when one feels responsible for someone else's untimely demise. Unfortunately that is where I fit into this particular story.

Looking back, that fateful day began like any other in my life as a teenager – calm and quiet. This was very different from a few months ago when my life was anything but typical. Six months earlier I frantically escaped my abusive childhood home and was placed in foster care. At this point, everything I did was a learning experience. No longer held hostage by my family, I eagerly tested my newfound wings. Until I ran away from home, my actions were tightly controlled; I had no freedom or friends. Finally liberated from overly confining parental restraints (and physical abuse) I thrived on making friends and enjoying new experiences. I was finally learning to be a normal teenager, not living the life of a prisoner convicted of a crime they didn't know they committed.

At this point my life was fairly topsy-turvy. I spent weekends at my foster home and during the week I was an inpatient at a psychiatric medical facility where therapists were helping me recover from post traumatic stress disorder. My admission took place in June and after three months of nearly complete seclusion I was eager to get out into the community but my particular circumstances did not allow it yet.

It was Friday and I had just come home from a week at the facility. I was upstairs unpacking my bags when the phone rang. Like any typical sixteen-year-old girl the phone was my umbilical cord to life. I eagerly stumbled down the stairs hoping the caller was looking for me. I was not disappointed. It was the daughter of the local minister.

When I arrived in my foster home several months earlier Candace was the first person my age who welcomed me to the neighborhood. Ours was a unique relationship – the preacher's daughter and the teen runaway! I was usually scorned by other kids my age, so it was hard to believe she wanted to be my friend and was not trying to convert me. But no matter what I told her about my childhood and the horrors I'd escaped from, she never seemed to judge me or my past.

"Want to come to Young Peoples with me tonight?" she asked. Young Peoples took place every Friday evening during the school year. Hosted by the local church, the group was open to local kids between grades 9 to 12. It was a great opportunity for me to meet other kids my age. I was curious but I was also frightened – my mother would never approve. Gatherings like this were foreign to me. I was raised Catholic and I was now living in a very Mennonite (Christian) community. My mother was adamant that we not mix with other religions because it might rub off of me. She always worried about me being converted and straying away from her beliefs. But in foster care, I was no longer under her control and the decision was completely mine.

"It's at the church, with other teenagers – you will have tons of fun," she explained to me, sensing my hesitation. She was soon assuring me it would be a harmless and fun evening. Shoving my mother's condemning voice to the back of my mind, I agreed. I didn't care about the church aspect but I did want to meet other kids.

"Hang on, let me ask," I covered the phone and called to my foster mother who was in the middle of making dinner. "Candace wants to know if I can come to church with her family tonight."

"Sure, I don't see anything wrong with that," my foster mother quickly agreed. Since my arrival in March she had been encouraging me to get out but I always hesitated. This was the first time I asked to attend an event with someone else my age since moving in.

"What time should I be ready?" I asked, returning my attention back to Candace.

"We leave here about 6:30," Candace responded. After promising to be ready in time, I hung up. I thanked my foster mother for giving me permission to go before heading back to my room, taking the stairs two at a time. Secretly, I was excited. Normally when I attended church, my mother would force me to wear a dress and cover my hair; wearing makeup was strictly forbidden. This night would be different. No longer confined to my mother's rules, I eagerly prepared for my 'debut'. I spent nearly an hour styling my hair and choosing my clothes. Everything had to be perfect for what I thought would be my big night.

Just before 7 o'clock I nervously descended the long flight stairs into the church basement where I came face-to-face with a room filled with strangers. All were teenagers around my age so I felt comfortable and yet, I was terrified. After being bullied at school for seven years, facing a group of kids who could also be my judgmental fellow classmates easily intimidated me. But that was quickly forgotten when the leaders Bev and Walter Flanders welcomed me warmly to the meeting. I had never felt such warmth from a group of strangers, in my entire life. My nervousness soon fled.

I sat through the program without really paying attention, while I covertly surveyed the crowd. I spotted a couple familiar faces from school a few months ago, but there was little real recognition. This eased my fear and boosted my confidence. At least for the evening, I was being noticed and welcomed instead of being forced to move around the room like a wraith.

After saying a few prayers and singing songs we were dismissed for a brief break before drinks and cookies were brought in. I searched the room for Candace but she looked busy. I scanned to room for other welcoming faces but everyone was occupied and I didn't want to interrupt. Noticing several people heading outside for fresh air, I eagerly bolted for the stairs. In some ways, I felt like a fish out of water. Smiling and pretending to fit in had taken a lot out of me and I needed a moment to recharge. When I got outside, I noticed a group of kids standing outside the door smoking. It struck me as comical that we were at church and the majority of the group was outside smoking cigarettes and talking about drinking parties. Spotting me, they called me over.

"Hey - you new here?" One boy asked, stating the obvious.

"Yes, I moved to Landmark a few months ago," I answered. He offered me a smoke, which I took even though I was not a smoker. As I puffed away he introduced himself before turning to introduce his buddies. I said hello to each but quickly forgot their names.

"Where do you live?" another boy asked. "How come we haven't seen you before?"

Having nothing to hide, I told them.

"I live on a little horse farm east of town," I eagerly answered. I wanted them to know that I would be around for awhile and was not just blowing through town. I didn't know how long I would be around but at this point even one friend would make the time less lonely.

"We know the place," a chorus of male voices responded. I was excited - a connection!

"Isn't that where Tanya lives?" One of the boys inquired. Tanya was one of my foster sisters. She'd lived in Landmark for a few years already and went to school with most of these kids.

"Yes, she's my foster sister," I hung my head in shame. Not because she was my foster sister but because I lived in a foster home. It was nearly as bad as admitting I was homeless.

"Where do you go to school?" another boy asked.

I could not answer that as easily. I had not attended school since before I ran away. As a matter of fact, my expulsion from school had led to my frantic escape from home. But I was not ready to share that information with these strangers.

"I don't go to school at the moment." I should have started classes in Landmark a few weeks earlier, but circumstances with Child and Family Services would delay my return to school for at least another year – but none of us knew that yet.

While we were chatting several more boys pulled into the church yard on dirt bikes and joined our group. It was obvious that everyone knew each other – most had been friends since before kindergarten. Being the new girl in the center of a group of handsome farm boys, I tried to be the life of the party. I wanted them to know who I was and remember meeting me. The way my circumstance's lay, who knew when I would next see these strapping lads. There was a lot of chatting and flirting going on and soon raging teen hormones gave way to reason. For once, instead of standing out, I fit right in and it was wonderful!

Time flew by and we never did go back inside the church for juice and cookies. We were having too much fun outside. It was a glorious September evening and the sun was just starting to set. The smell of freshly combined fields hung in the air. It was a lovely evening and the boys wanted to go out and play.

At one point this very tall boy wandered over and introduced himself as Henry. He told me he lived in a tiny hamlet a few miles west. He asked if I had ever been there. I admitted I had, but I didn't know where he lived.

"You should come over sometime," he suggested. I already knew it would be impossible; my foster parents monitored me closely and allowing me to wander off with a boy was not on the agenda. I may have been sixteen but I was not emotionally ready to date. But that didn't mean I couldn't have fun.

"It's getting dark, I should go home soon," he said. Looking around I noted that dusk was starting to fall.

"That your bike?" I asked, pointing to one of the dirt bikes propped up in the lot. I had enjoyed our conversation and I didn't want him to leave just yet.

"Yep, and I should be heading home," Henry continued. "Have you ever been on one?"

My older brother had dirt bikes when I was growing up but I had never been one before; but I was not going to admit that.

"Want to go for a little ride?" he asked. I may have just met Henry but he seemed harmless. I tried to rationalize the situation, weighing the pros (the ride) and cons (the punishment I could face for taking the ride) and decided the risk was worth the possible punishment. What the heck, why not, who would we hurt? But I still hesitated.

"Tell you what, I just live down the road, let's go for a little ride and I will show you my house; that way you can come visit me when you have a chance," he offered with a welcoming smile. I looked at my watch. It was getting late and I was afraid my ride would leave without me.

"Hang on, I have to see when we are leaving." He nodded in agreement and I dashed into the church to find my ride. She was talking to some of her classmates when I found her.

"Are you having fun?" she asked, after introducing me to her friends.

"Yes, I just met Henry and some other boys," I volunteered. "Are we going to be awhile yet?"

"Dad still has some work to do so it could be another hour or so," she answered. "Why?"

"The guys are outside and Henry wants to take me for a dirt bike ride, I've never been on one." Telling my friend, I grew more excited.

"So go, just be back here by 10PM," Candace offered. She looked happy to know that I had connected with a few people. Before she could change her mind, I dashed back outside.

"So, you ready to go for a little spin?" Henry asked as he tossed the cigarette butt across the parking lot.

"Yep, as long we don't go too far, I am good to go." I was feeling uneasy, but I chalked it up to inexperience and shook it off. I was also nervous about being alone with a boy and I wasn't going to admit that either.

"Like I said, I live only two miles down the road — we will be there and back before you know it." He sounded so sure of himself I was compelled to trust him. I followed him to the bike and waited as he kicked started it to life. I stayed out of the way. My brother's dirt bike would only start if he held on and ran beside it until it fired. Once it was running, Henry moved forward onto the one-person seat and patted a spot behind him. Trying to appear fearless and experienced I climbed up and wrapped my arms around him tightly.

"You ready?" He asked, thumbing the throttle with impatience. I nodded. There was no passenger pegs so I had to place my feet on where his should be. At one point, my foot slipped and hit the hot muffler. I squelched my yelp; I would check to see how bad the burn was later. It was not very comfortable and I hoped the ride would be as short as he promised. Before I could protest we peeled out of the church parking lot.

On the highway, the evening was much darker than it appeared while we were standing outside the church. The fading harvest moon cast an eerie light on the blacktop highway. I held on tight, as Henry turned west and kicked the bike's speed up a notch. It wasn't until we got further out of town and away from the streetlights that I noticed the bike had no headlights. I started to get nervous as we sped through the darkness at what I considered a dangerous speed. I clutched onto him tightly, at the same time regretting being so impetuous.

It didn't seem like we had gone very far down the highway when the pavement turned into gravel. Without headlights or streetlights as guides, we had drifted onto the shoulder and were heading towards disaster. Henry must have sensed my inexperience. Instead of steering the bike back onto the road, he let it gently roll down into a deep ditch. Our momentum kept us moving until we finally coasted to a stop in a farmer's field. When we stopped moving, I put my feet down. In my thin sneakers I could make out the furrows.

"Oops – I guess we got off track," Henry laughed said as he climbed off the bike. "Hang on a sec, let me turn this baby around and then we will get back onto the road."

I was starting to feel nervous, but I managed a gruff "okay" and a brief nod. Satisfied, he quickly got on then gunned the bike around to face the road then patted the seat.

"Get on and hold on tight!" He shouted as he gunned the engine a few times.

Swallowing my budding fear, I climbed back on and hung on for dear life. The bike suddenly lurched up the embankment and we were back on the highway. Despite my false bravado, I was relieved to be back on solid ground again. Heading westward our nervous laughter was lost in the night as we continued our adventure. The night was glorious and I was enjoying the wind whipping at my hair and the freedom of speeding off into the darkness. I had never felt so alive and thrilled.

The dirt bike wasn't built for two and I could tell that Henry was concentrating on keeping us on the highway. It was obvious that neither of us wanted to end up back in the middle of the field, so I kept an eye out for any hazards. Somewhere in my peripheral vision I caught a flicker of lights. I looked over my shoulder and in the furtive glance I spotted headlights. They were coming quickly behind us; cutting the darkness like a knife.

I turned and started to nudge Henry, trying to warn him that we had company.

"I think there is a car coming!" The words had barely escaped my lips when something hit us from behind. Our bike skid sideways from the impact. While the bike slid along the pavement, our bodies took to the sky. I was airborne for moments, but an eternity flashed before me. *I am going to die. Lord, don't let this be it.* I prayed as I slid across the pavement. It is amazing how those few seconds seem to go by in slow motion and more thoughts than you can imagine possible can surface in those precious moments. I had enough time to put out my arms in a feeble attempt to keep my face from hitting the highway. I barely noticed the burning sensation in my right arm where the skin was stripped off by the cold black asphalt during my fall. I lay there a few moments trying to catch my breath and bearings. *I was alive!*

Wrapped in shock and pain, I lifted my head and barely understood the highway was mere millimeters from the tip of my nose. I had to get up. Trying to move, a sharp pain ripped through my ankle. It was then I noticed I was missing a shoe. Tears were streaming down my face when I finally managed to peel myself off the ground. The night was so still. Even the crickets had gone silent.

I peered into the night, hoping to see if whoever had hit us had stopped to see if we were okay. But no taillights could be seen at any direction. There was nothing but silent darkness. Whatever hit us was no longer there.

"You okay?" I heard Henry ask. I didn't hear or see him rush over. I couldn't see his face but I could tell by his voice that he was shaken. I was also relieved that he was okay.

"I am so sorry, I don't know what happened." He looked terrified.

"Yes, I think so – where is my shoe?" I took a few limping test steps; my ankle was screaming in pain. I was starting to panic. "We need to go back NOW," I was nearing hysterics and sobbing even harder. Trying to calm me, Henry gathered me into his arms.

"It's okay, it will be okay – I am so sorry," he kept repeating over and over while I trembled in his arms. When he finally pushed me away, he went to find my shoe. I could not make out anything in the dark. It was as if the flash of head-light or whatever it was I saw had blinded me temporarily. While Henry searched for our shoes – he'd lost his too - he tried to reassure me. I couldn't see him but I could hear him stumbling around in the darkness. Finally, he found it and returned to my side.

"We have to go back," he barked. "Are you okay to ride?" He didn't wait for me to answer. Righting the bike, he gave it a quick once over in the darkness. When he was satisfied that it would get us back, he pushed to leave immediately.

"I can't – I am going to walk back. I can't get back onto that thing." I was terrified to get back on after the spill we just took. To prove my point, I started walking back in the direction we had just come. I had already spotted a nearby farm and was more than prepared to walk down their driveway and get a ride. Henry stopped me.

"No – you are hurt; you won't make it because it is too far to walk. We have to get back to the church and get help." I knew he was right – my ride would be waiting for us. I had lost track of time and it seemed like we had been gone for hours.

"Listen, I know you are scared but we have to get back. Trust me, I will be careful," Henry promised. Afraid he might leave me behind, I stopped arguing. I felt like I had just cheated death. This was my first "close call". Despite my fear, I pulled up my pants and climbed back onto the bike. We were soon heading back to the church as quick as possible while I tried not to panic. After what we'd just been though, the last thing he needed was a crazy girl throwing his balance off.

A deep sigh escaped me, along with my pent-up tears when the church finally came into sight. I fought back tears of relief. As we pulled into the driveway, the majority of the group was already gathered outside. Some kids were waiting for their rides and others were just visiting with classmates.

"Hey – get over here," Henry yelled at the group as we drew adjacent to the door. But instead of pulling the bike up to the door, where help was already unknowingly waiting, he steered the bike towards the back of the building. We must have looked like hell because there was no hesitation – everyone came running.

He'd barely stopped when two pairs of arms grabbed onto me, while Henry steadied the bike. There was a lot of confusion and I vaguely remember him telling the guys we'd been in an accident. A hit-and-run, he said. I blubbered something about thinking it was a car that sped away in the darkness. All three boys helped me hobble back to the front of the church, just as the adults were coming out. Our arrival had caused a commotion and word had already spread that we had been in an accident.

Finally safe and in the care of other adults, the adrenaline rush wore off and my body began to throb. Bearing weight on my ankle was impossible, and the shock on the night set in. Uncontrollable trembling took over as I was placed into the minister's car. I would have preferred to leave immediately but the minister went back to talk to Henry. I couldn't hear the exchange but I assume he wanted some answers. They didn't talk too long.

We were soon on the road and heading back to my foster home. Knowing that I would soon be home, I curled up into the backseat of the car and tried not to think about the pain I was in. By this time, my arm was on fire and blood pooled on my fingertips. I couldn't see the damage yet, but I was starting to feel it. Limiting my movement help me control the pain. I couldn't wait to crawl into my bed and forget about the night.

AFTERMATH

A mile from the church, we were pulling up to the corner stop sign when a car came screaming up from behind us. I was still very jumpy so the blaring car horn startled me. At first I thought the driver was trying to signal us to pull over. We started to pull over to the shoulder, but before the minister could stop the little Honda civic swerved around us with hazard lights flashing and horn blaring. The driver barely slowed down as he made the corner and headed towards Steinbach. The car vanished into the night as quickly as it had arrived.

"Someone is sure in a hurry to get somewhere fast," commented the Minister before continuing down the gravel road.

When we pulled into the driveway, the house was ablaze with light. Someone had already notified my foster family and briefly updated them on what happened. Not only were they waiting for an explanation but we had yet to determine the extent of my injuries. My foster father met us at the car and helped me inside.

"What happened?" He asked. The minister quickly filled in my foster mother with the little details he knew. I sat in a stunned silence. It was finally hitting me how close I had come to death. When you think about it, we were both ill prepared for the ride. Neither one of us were wearing helmets, I was wearing wool and sneakers. To this day, I cringe when I see riders wearing shorts and runners while on a motorcycle.

Then there was the fact my family was unaware of the incident. My mother would freak if she knew how irresponsible I was. I felt a lot of shame, but that was soon forgotten as my foster mother began in inspect my wounds. Used to tending equine injuries, I trusted my foster mother's medical expertise. A quick once-over revealed my red and black jack-shirt was embedded in my skin. Its affect on my arm was similar to rug-burn, with an added mixture of fabric and gravel. My hand was also skinned; the flesh was barely hanging in along my right pinky finger.

The more I sat, the harder it got to remain mobile. Walking was impossible at this point. My right ankle had swollen to twice its normal size. It was also starting to turn a hideous purple. Even if no bones were broken, my other wounds needed a good cleaning. I was unaware of the fact that Child and Family Services required a full report on the incident for my records, which was another reason I needed to be seen by a doctor. I was given something mild for pain before the men carried me to the car. Within minutes we were on our way to the Ste. Anne Hospital. On the way, I filled in my foster family on what had happened.

The rest of the night was a fog. At some point a kindly nurse gave me a shot in my hip to help with the pain. I am assuming it was Demoral or something similar. I vaguely recall being rolled into X-ray, where images were taken of my arm and my ankle. The only reason I remember it, was the excruciating pain I experienced whenever the nurse moved my damaged limbs one way or the other to get a better picture. Examination revealed that nothing was broken, but I was missing a lot of skin along my right side. Before the needle, the pain was unbearable.

At this point, I am glad the nurses drugged me. I had gravel imbedded deeply in my skin, pavement fragments, and wool fabric fibers. Each one had to be removed with a pair of tweezers. Of course the wound would bleed and a healthy dose of peroxide was applied. I think I eventually passed out from the pain. Although I am sure I was also in shock.

Finally around two o'clock in the morning I was rolled into recovery for "observation". This was my first night in a hospital since my tonsillectomy at seven. Content that I would be fine, my foster family eventually went home. I soon fell into a drug induced sleep, only to stir when the nurses checked on me every few hours.

Around mid-morning, the doctor gave me the okay to go home. My foster family arrived, and after a hurried lesson with crutches, I was sent on my way. I was happy to be on my way home and looking forward to crawl into my own bed. On the way back, the car was quiet - almost too quiet.

"I am sorry about last night," I muttered. Once the words were spilled, it was easy to repeat them. "I don't know what happened – but I am sorry for all this trouble."

I genuinely felt bad. No matter how my foster family tried to make me feel like I fit in, I still felt like a nuisance. I was well aware that I was not family - I was a temporary house quest. I tried to be low maintenance and I obeyed their rules. I learned a long time ago that rules had to be followed or there were dire consequences. I had finally found a home; I didn't want to lose it. And here I was, on one of my few weekends home, and I end up in an accident with a bunch of boys during a harmless church event. I had broke their trust, and to me that was unforgiveable.

"What do you remember?" My foster mother asked hesitantly. I was trying to apologize and they wanted more information. I was not sure what this meant.

I repeated my story, trying to remember things I didn't mention the previous night due to my physical circumstances. I tried not to leave out a single detail. It helped to talk about it, it helped me remember. I still couldn't believe I was okay. Silence followed my reflections. The vehicle's speed had also decreased during my recollection.

"We need to tell you something," my foster father started to speak. I could see him watching me in the rear view mirror. I could tell that something was bothering him and he was trying to find the right words. I waited in silence.

After a pregnant pause, my foster mother piped in. "You need to know the police will be at the house when we get there. They want a statement from you about the accident."

"The police?"

I wasn't surprised that I would have to give a statement. I didn't know who reported the accident, and just assumed the hospital had notified the RCMP when I was admitted. It was not urgent so they wouldn't have bothered to come see me in the hospital. Believing it was a hit-and-run, this made sense to me. They would want information to find out who did it, just in case.

"Yes, the police want to talk to you. There is something you need to know though, before we go in. You need to hear this from us, not the police." My foster mother's voice failed. I could tell she was having a hard time, searching for the right words. When she finally found them, I was dumbfounded. "Someone died last night." I was confused. I was here, and the last time I saw Henry he didn't have a scratch on him. Who could have died?

"Someone died? But we were both fine."

"No, you don't understand – there was someone else in the accident."

Once again, I was confused. Now that was an idea I had not even considered. This entire time, I had just assumed we were struck by a car, and it sped off into the night. The thought of someone else there, just did not make sense. I would have noticed something – anything.

"Did you see anything, anything at all?" My foster father pressed. I was positive I did not see anything. I remember standing on the yellow line, peering westward but not seeing anything in the distance. There should have been a set of tail lights. Someone should have stopped – but no one was there.

Too stunned to do anything other than sob I shook my head no. I was positive on that point. From my vantage, there had been nothing around us, but dark night and distant houselights.

By this time, we were pulling into the driveway and two police cars were already waiting. I was suddenly terrified. I didn't know what to expect, I just knew I had to tell the truth. I was hustled into the house and sat down in the kitchen. Once I was comfortable an officer entered the room and began his questioning.

For the second time that morning, I repeated everything that happened the night before while the officer scribbled on some forms. We had to pause a few times to get the details right. I didn't know why, but I knew it was important. When we were done, he handed them over to me to re-read and then sign. My sworn statement on the matter, I was told.

The last page signed, I mustering up courage to ask the officer for details on what they thought happened that night. I was told my statement was the missing piece of the puzzle, and with all the statements (I am assuming Henry's and other witnesses at the church) taken I felt safe in asking the officers to tell me what they found.

The officer relayed brief but concise details of the accident and I started sobbing. I tuned out his exact words, desperately hoping they were not real. My sixteen-year-old already wounded mind could not comprehend the guilt over my seemingly selfish actions.

As I suspected, according to the officer, we were hit by another motor-vehicle. While I was looking for duel taillights, we were actually hit from behind by another dirt bike. This was Brian. He had just left the church and was heading for home, where his mother, father and brothers were waiting. Four more miles and he would have been safe in his bed.

While we felt our way along the highway through the darkness without a headlight or taillight, Brian was creeping up behind us. He had a headlight on the front of his bike. That was the light I saw before I was flying through the air. Based on the skid-marks at the scene, he must have caught us in the beam of his headlight just before his front tire hit our back tire. He didn't have enough time to react. The impact sent us into a skid, while he was vaulted over his handlebars; crashing hard onto the shoulder of the highway.

Slowly, the pieces of the puzzle began to fit. It hit me that while I was sobbing, shoeless along the yellow centerline, Brian was lying broken and dying along the side of the road.

"I swear I didn't know," I silently bawled. "I didn't know, I didn't know." It became a chant inside my head. Echoing, tuning out everything around me. Eventually I tuned back into the conversation to hear more details.

The officer further confirmed the car that passed us in such a hurry was carrying Brian's dying body to the Steinbach hospital miles away. The driver was on his way home from work when he spotted something on the side of the road. Stopping his vehicle, he went to investigate and found both Brian along the side of the road. His broken dirt bike lie a few feet away. It was the sudden movement by the Good Samaritan that probably killed Brian, added the officer. When I became a paramedic later in life, I learned the importance of stabilization when a neck injury is suspected. A patient is immobilized and even the slightest movement can sever the spinal cord. A broken neck could have left him disabled, but not dead - if he had not been moved.

As the officer's words sank in, the impact of responsibility settled on me like a ton of bricks. If these boys had not been showing off, they would not have been so reckless. Scores of "what-ifs" flowed from my lips like tears. My face was soaked from the downpour originating from my eyes and ultimately my soul. I mourned for a life lost so young. My young heart was broken.

Based on my statement, Henry was never charged for the accident. Legally, I think that was a good decision. After further investigation and talking to the immediate families on both sides, the RCMP ruled the accident as a "tragedy". But that doesn't mean he didn't pay the price. You would think an incident such as this would draw two people together. For us, we avoided the topic. I ran into him over the years; he was always a wreck. I cannot imagine the horror he felt. I also forgot he was only fifteen at the time too. We were all young and reckless.

While I have carried this burden in my heart for decades, very few people actually know I was there that night. Publicly, I was the unknown female youth. Henry's burden was worse. Small towns are cruel and I know many people suspected he may have deliberately walked away from the scene. The local rumor mill speculated that was the reason he headed behind the church, instead of to the front door.

I choose to believe that he didn't know. I would never ask. That is between him and God. We were young, panicked and in a situation that could have cost us our lives. For me, the hardest part was that Henry lost his best friend that night. The two boys were neighbors and inseparable. I cannot imagine his pain, even without the other drama.

As for me, I wore my remorse like a thick blanket. My physical wounds would eventually heal, but my heart remained heavy with guilt. It would be decades before I climbed onto a motorcycle too. The one thing that made it worse was being raised to believe that I was an abomination. My mother was vicious sometimes and she had me believing that bad things happened to people around me which is why people avoided me. In my messed up state of mind, I genuinely believed I caused the accident, and to avoid other such incidents, I had to avoid people at all costs. Eliminate the problem and the world remains safe.

I welcomed physical pain – my wounds were not healing very well. Ste. Anne Hospital gauzed me up and sent me on my way. It wasn't until a few days later, staff at the treatment facility I was staying at started to notice a peculiar odor coming from my arm. After a quick check, it was determined my dressing had not been changed since I was admitted – almost a week earlier. The bandages had to come off. Easier said than done; as layer after layer of gauze peeled off, it was soon obvious that my arm was infected and the gauze was not coming easy. It took three hours of soaking in a warm bath of peroxide to get the pus scabs to let go. Even then, my screams could be heard throughout the facility as the nurses eventually had to just peel it off. There was no time to be gentle. I welcomed the agony. It reminded me about how lucky I was.

It would also be months before I ride in the passenger seat of a car without curling up in a ball on the floor if we were driving after dusk. I would freak out and have a panic attack every time I saw a headlights coming towards us. My foster father showed a lot of patience towards me during that time. When I was not on the floor, I was usually screaming in fear. I had a hard time recovering.

I eventually found closure in the form of a letter that I penned to Brian's mother. A year after the accident I was compelled to contact her. I wanted her to know how sorry I was; that while I didn't know her son, I had met him that night and I was sorry I would never get to know how great he was. My tears mingled with blue ink as I apologized for my part in her youngest son's death. In the words of a mature sixteen year old I wrote that if I could change, I would. With its mailing, I closed the chapter on that horrific night.

Around the one year anniversary of the accident, Brian's mother found that letter waiting in her mailbox.

HEALING HEARTS

Two years later on my wedding day, I was standing in the presentation line when I was approached by a sweet looking older lady. While I didn't know her name but I knew she was invited because of her connection to my new husband's family.

"This is Mrs. Kauenhofen," my husband said as he introduced us. "She lives on the chicken farm near my parents place." It took me a few seconds to make the connection. My eyes widened as she congratulated me.

My husband's words sank in – Mrs. Kauenhofen – I knew that name. I paled. Her face betrayed recognition also. She knew who I was. I waited for the coming condemnation. I expected her to yell at me, scream at me – something. How fitting this confrontation take place at my wedding – something her son would never have. Whatever I was expecting never came. Instead, she reached for me and I allowed her to take my hands in hers. Ashamed, I attempted to return her gaze. My heart was quaking.

"I got your letter," I watched her lips, not hearing her words. Somehow my flustered brain registered the sincerity in her face. She was not angry. She actually looked happy to see me. I noted the tears threatening to spill over, to join mine. The wait seemed like an eternity. Yet, it lasted only seconds. As she took me into her arms in a warm forgiving embrace, I heard her whisper.

"Thank you for your letter," she said. "You were the only one – other than family - who remembered the night that Brian died. You have no idea how much that letter meant to us. Thank you."

Her words rained down on me like a blessing. The forgiving peace I desperately sought since that night was finally achieved with whispered words. After years of nightmares, and misguided guilt over taking another's life, even accidentally – I felt relief. Her simple soft-spoken words gave my broken heart permission to heal. In the wake of a grieving mother's forgiving words I was finally able to do something I never thought that I could do. I was finally able to forgive myself for the night that Brian took his last ride.

Authors Note:

I had a recent opportunity to speak to "Henry" – and he was very grateful for the communication. The one thing he wanted to thank me for, was finally setting him straight on one thing – in nearly thirty years, he was never told the actual cause of death. For some reason, knowing what actually happened has finally allowed him to find closure for himself.

I am grateful to God for presenting me with this opportunity to remember a life lost too soon.

ABOUT THE AUTHOR

Since the fall of 1997, Marianne Curtis has been writing for the Dawson Trail Dispatch. She has since published over 7,000 articles in the monthly publication.

While she prefers investigative pieces, Ms. Curtis does not limit her expertise. Over the years she has covered hardcore news, political issues, public interest groups, community events, sports and entertainment. She also does her own photography.

When Ms. Curtis is not writing for the newspaper, she enjoys spending time with her family, gardening and with her many friends.

Contact the Author
mariannecurtis.author@gmail.com

Made in the USA
Monee, IL
07 July 2026